But What If...

Paula Nagel

Illustrated by Gary Bainbridge

First published 2017
by Routledge
2 Park Square, Milton Park, Abingdon, Oxon OX14 4RN

and by Routledge
711 Third Avenue, New York, NY 10017

Routledge is an imprint of the Taylor & Francis Group, an informa business

© 2017 Paula Nagel
Illustrations copyright © 2017 Gary Bainbridge

British Library Cataloguing-in-Publication Data
A catalogue record for this book is available from the British Library

Library of Congress Cataloging-in-Publication Data
A catalog record for this book has been requested.

ISBN: 978 1 90930 176 4 (pbk)
ISBN: 978 131517 501 0 (ebk)

Typeset in Univers Light Condensed
by Moo Creative (Luton)

Visit the eResources: www.routledge.com/9781909301764

MIX
Paper from
responsible sources
FSC
www.fsc.org   FSC® C013604   Printed and bound by CPI Group (UK) Ltd, Croydon, CRO 4YY

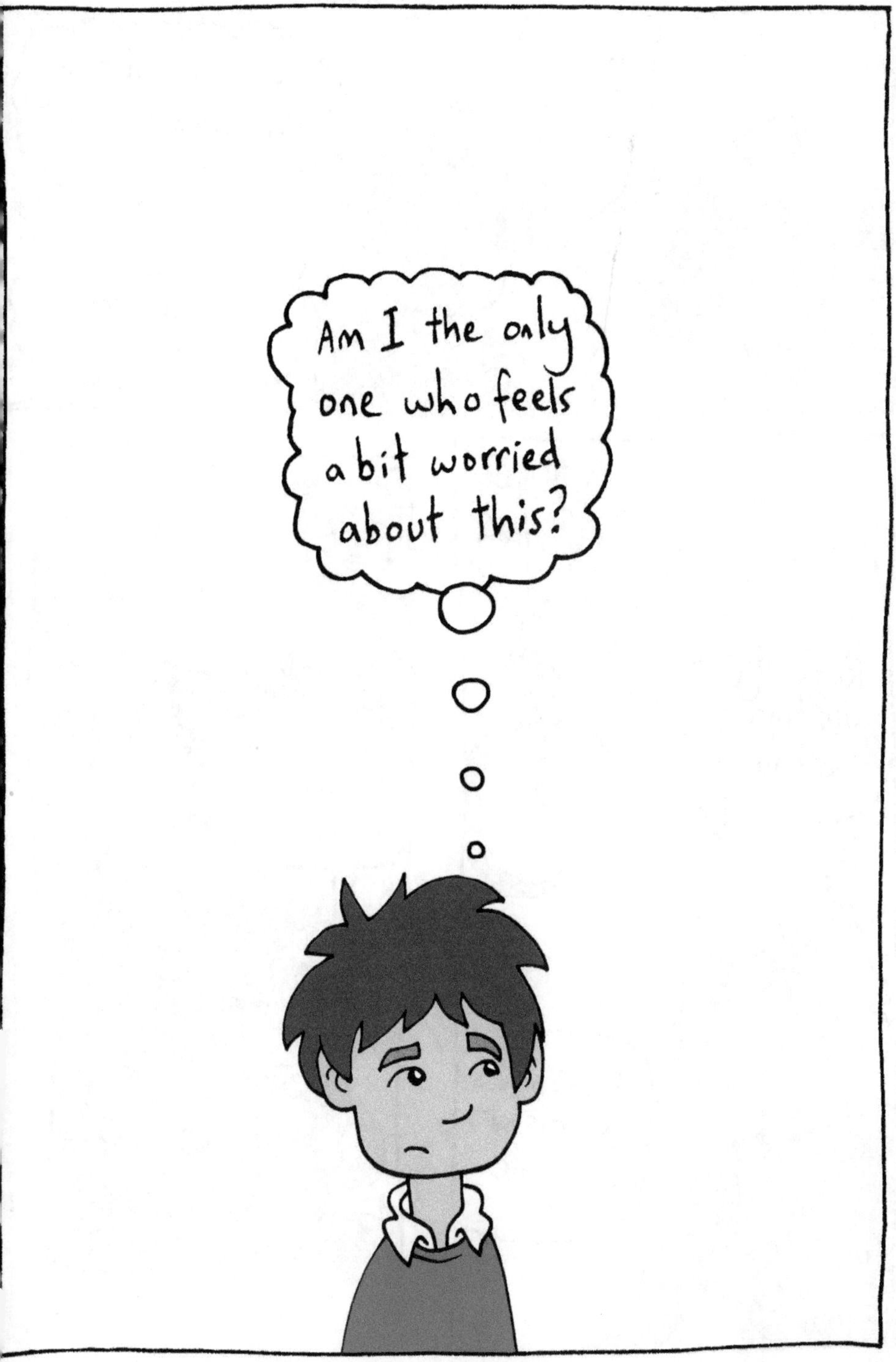
Am I the only one who feels a bit worried about this?

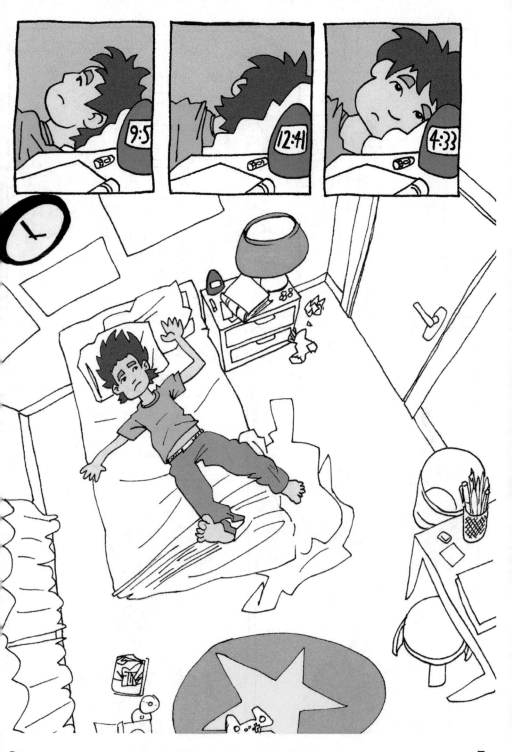

Yes, all of those things, and funnily enough, some of the things you look forward to might be the things that worry you at the same time.

Ding Ding!

Have you heard any...

You know... rumours about Redbridge?

Rumours? Like what?

Well you know.

That it's ginormous.

They say the place is like a maze, and you can totally get lost in it.

Oh yeah.

Like that Year 7 girl last year.

...

Yeah, you know the one that got lost for a **week**.

They had to call the cops to find her.

Naaa...

It's not **that** big...

It is, my brother told me. Don't worry though-- you get a map.

Yeah I guess so. But what if you lose it?

But What If? Workbook 1

Let's talk about ... worry and change

Here's Jake to share some of the things he learned about worry and change.

We all worry.

It's normal to feel worried from time to time. There are all sorts of things that can make us worried.

Write or draw some of the things that have made you feel worried on these worry weeds.

Worry can be a big feeling and it can be helpful.

When you feel threatened by something, worry can help you to get ready to face that threat.

It does this by making your heart beat faster and pumping blood around your body, making you feel alert, full of energy and ready to do your best.

But sometimes worry grows quickly, just like a weed in the garden.

Sometimes worry becomes such a big feeling that it leaves no space for anything else.

Sometimes worry grows so big that it can change your behaviour and stop you from doing the things you usually like to do.

Look again at my story and see if you can spot how my big worry feelings stopped me from doing things I enjoy and how it changed my behaviour.

Now make your own comic strip of this in the spaces below.

Some of the things that make us worry involve change.

Changing schools is one of the things that can cause big worry feelings.

Can you remember the things my friends and I worried about?

Look back at my story and draw or write our worries on the worry weeds below.

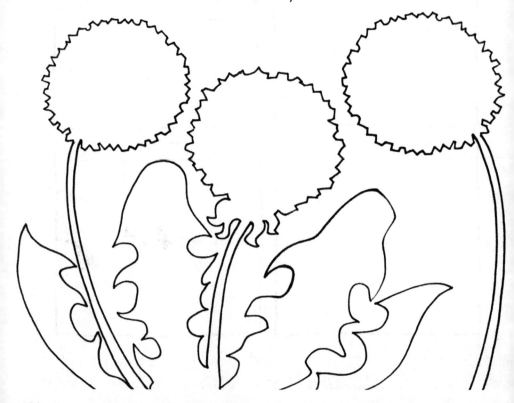

I didn't share my worry and it grew
bigger and **bigger**.

Worry needs to be kept under control –
just like a weed.

What makes worry wither?

Worry likes to grow unnoticed – just like a weed
Here are some ideas about how to stop the worr
weed from growing so **big** that it takes over.

Read them and try them out for yourself.

1 Keep a watchful eye on the worry weed. Notice the worry and how it can take up all of the thoughts in your mind.

Thoughts about worry kept popping into my mind, even when I was trying to do other things like watch television or sleep.

It's normal for worry to pop into your head ...

Sometimes just noticing that worry is there can help to stop it growing.

2 Notice the worry and how it makes your body feel.

Look back at the things on your worry weeds.

Pick one worry and try to remember if you noticed it in your body.

- Perhaps it was in your stomach?
- In your breathing?
- Maybe it made you feel hot or cold?
- Did it make your muscles tense?
- Did it make your legs or hands shake?

Write an 'X' on the places where you have noticed worry in your body.

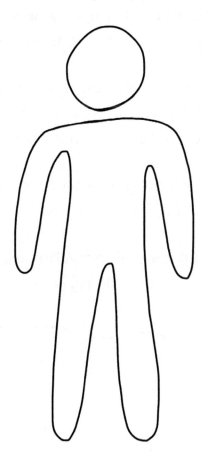

If you can't remember where you felt the worry, try to watch out for it the next time you feel worried.

3 Keep on doing the things you enjoy.

Lots of things can make worry wither, including doing the things you enjoy.

Even if you don't always feel like it, try to keep on doing the things you enjoy, to stop **big** worry feelings taking over.

I will try to keep on going to football practice, especially when I have big worry feelings.

What do you enjoy doing? What will you try to keep doing?

4 Talking about worry can make it wither.

Sharing the worry with another person is like digging it out from the roots.

Who can you talk to when you are feeling worried?

Draw them or write their names below.

5 Don't water the worry weed.

Weeds need water to grow.
Sometimes our thoughts about things can
make worry grow.

These are **unhelpful thoughts**.

Unhelpful thoughts can water the worry weed.

Unhelpful thoughts often start with the words '**But What If**...?' and end with the worst thing you can think of.

Here are some of my unhelpful thoughts.

But what if I ask about the toilets? ... then everyone will think I am stupid.

But what if I lose my map? ... then I'll get lost for a week.

But what if everyone finds out about my worry? ... then I'll be one big joke.

But what if I go to the toilet? ... then I'll get my head flushed.

Unhelpful thoughts focus on the bad things and ignore all of the good things.

Sometimes they exaggerate the bad things and make them seem even worse.

Look back at my story and spot when my unhelpful thoughts made things seem even worse.

Unhelpful thoughts water the worry weed.

I emptied my watering can of **unhelpful thoughts** by testing them.

Here's how I tested my **unhelpful thoughts**.

I asked myself ... Is this thought a fact?

Remember: facts have proof that they are true.

Unhelpful thoughts often don't have any proof and are not facts.

Unhelpful thought

Everyone will think I am one big joke.

Is this a fact? Do I have any proof that it is true?

No. I can't read their minds and know what they are thinking.

This is **not a fact**.

I changed my unhelpful thought into a more helpful one like this ...

Not everyone will think I am a joke. And if someone does call me a joke, it's not the end of the world. I can ignore them or choose not to talk to them. My real friends won't think I am a joke.

See if you can test some of my unhelpful thoughts.

But what if I get lost? Then they won't find me for a week!

Is this a fact? Does it have any proof?
This is **not a fact**. This is an **unhelpful thought** and does not have any proof.

I have no proof that anyone has ever been lost for a week. **I don't know for sure that I will get lost.**

I might get lost ... but then again, I might not.

I changed my unhelpful thought into a more helpful one like this ...

I might get lost in my new school but there will be lots of other Year 7 students who might also be lost and we can all help each other.

If I get lost, I can use my map, ask another pupil or find an adult. It's not likely that I will get lost in school for a whole week.

My mum would miss me if I didn't come home, or the caretaker would help me find my way out.

Getting lost for a week is a rumour to scare new starters.

Can you test this next thought?

If I go to the toilets, I will get my head flushed.

Is there any proof for this thought?
Is this thought a fact?
Try changing it into a more helpful thought.

Remember! Worry doesn't stay the same for ever.

Write or draw about the worry in a notebook or a worry diary.

My worry diary

What makes me worry? – going to big school

Where I notice the worry – in my tummy – I get a wobbly feeling and sometimes a pain

My unhelpful thoughts – what if I get lost? What if I get my head flushed?

What can I do? – test my worrying thoughts

Relax my body by listening to my favourite songs

Do things I enjoy, like playing football and being with my friends

Share the worry by talking about it

Summary

Remember: it is normal to feel worried from time to time.

Worry can grow and become a big feeling.

But worry usually goes away once you notice it and talk about it.

Don't ignore the worry weed.

Notice it and keep a watchful eye on it, tell someone about it and keep on doing the things you enjoy.

However, if worry doesn't go away, you might need some more help to make it wither.
Tell someone how it is affecting you straight away.